Murray

NATURE ATTACKS!

ALSO BY LAUREN TARSHIS

NATURE ATTACKS!

Lauren Tarshis

SCHOLASTIC INC.

ISBN 978-0-545-90802-3

10 9 8 7 6 5 4 3 2   15 16 17 18 19

Printed in the U.S.A.   23

First edition 2015

Book design by Deborah Dinger and Yaffa Jaskoll

For Andrew

CONTENTS

AUTHOR'S NOTE

Hello to you!

I'm so happy that you have decided to read this second collection of I Survived True Stories. In many ways, the stories you are about to read here are just like the books in my I Survived series. They are exciting (at least I hope they are!). They required tons of research. They are about topics that are fascinating and terrifying.

But my I Survived books are historical fiction. While they are all based on true events, the characters and other details in those books are fictional. The True Stories collections, on the other hand, are works of nonfiction. That means that not only are the events true, but the characters are real kids just like you.

I was writing nonfiction articles a long time

before I ever had the idea for I Survived. In fact, I still write nonfiction stories every month for the magazine I edit, *Scholastic Storyworks*. This amazing magazine is read by about 900,000 kids, mostly in grades four and five. For years, the most popular *Storyworks* feature has been a long nonfiction story, usually focused on a real-life child who is smack in the middle of an important historic event or natural disaster. Many of these articles focus on the same subjects that I tackle in my I Survived books—shipwrecks, natural disasters, thrilling historical events, or confrontations between people and deadly animals.

After I started writing the I Survived series, I realized that you readers would probably love these nonfiction stories, too. That's what gave me the idea to create these True Stories collections.

In the following stories, you're going to meet four incredible kids. Each faced one of nature's most powerful and ferocious forces. There's Joseph

Dunn, who had a terrifying encounter with a massive shark in a New Jersey creek. There's John Hoisington, whose family experienced the deadly effects of the Mount Tambora volcanic eruption, one of history's most powerful. You'll meet John Kramer, who faced the Peshtigo fire, the deadliest in American history. And finally there's amazing Rachael Shardlow, who was stung by the venomous box jellyfish.

I feel so lucky that my work takes me to such fascinating places and introduces me to people who stay in my heart and mind long after I finish writing about them. I hope you are as inspired by these true stories as I am.

Happy reading adventures!

#1

SUMMER OF TERROR

THE TRUE STORY OF THE
SHARK ATTACKS OF 1916

It was July 12, 1916, and twelve-year-old Joseph Dunn was sprinting toward Matawan Creek. Behind him were his fourteen-year-old brother, Michael, and their buddy Jerry Hollohan. It was a wild race to get into the water, and Joe was determined to win.

They reached the dock and Joe leaped off.

Splash!

Joe hit the cool water, sinking down, down, down. He let his toes touch the mucky bottom before blasting himself back up with a splash.

What could be better than this?

Joe and Michael lived in New York City, but they came out to Cliffwood, New Jersey, as often as they could. Their aunt lived there, and lucky for Joe and Michael, she was always happy to have them. The tiny town of Cliffwood wasn't a fancy place, not like those towns on the south New Jersey shore where rich people went for the summer. There were no hotels, no white-sand beaches with pounding waves. Matawan Creek was a muddy waterway whose banks were lined with brick and tile factories.

During the hot summer of 1916, New York City kids find cool relief in a fountain.

But to Joe and Michael, Cliffwood was paradise, a happy escape from the misery of summer in New York City.

It was blazing hot up and down the East Coast—nobody could remember such brutal heat so early in the summer. The heat wave brought particular suffering to city dwellers, and not just the humans. In New York City and Philadelphia, horses fainted in the streets. Dogs yelped in pain as they walked along the stove-hot sidewalks. Even the cockroaches in the Dunns' roasting apartment seemed to drag in the stifling air.

Out in Cliffwood, Joe and Michael could forget all about that. They could play pickup baseball games with Jerry and other local kids. They could buy nickel ice-cream cones on Main Street. And best of all, they could always cool off in the creek.

Joe was looking forward to an afternoon of swimming and racing with the guys. But their carefree mood was interrupted by the sound of a voice shouting at them to get out of the water.

A man appeared on the dock, sweat-soaked and out of breath.

The look on his face sent chills down Joe's spine.

He looked terrified. And what he said next nearly stopped Joe's heart.

"There's a shark in the creek!"

A shark? In the creek?

Before Joe could even get his mind around such a horrifying idea, he was swimming frantically toward shore. He made it to the dock, where Michael and Jerry were already out of the water. Michael reached out to help Joe climb up, but before Joe could lift his legs onto the ladder, a dark shape suddenly appeared in the water next to him.

Seconds later, Joe felt something grab hold of his leg, like a giant pair of scissors.

He felt a crunch. The water around him suddenly turned bright red.

A great
white shark
shows off
its powerful
jaws.

Joe opened his mouth, but he was too terrified to even scream. Time seemed to slow, and everything around him went dim.

Joseph Dunn was about to become a victim of one of the most notorious series of shark attacks in history—the shark attacks of 1916. By the time the terror was over, three men and one boy would be dead.

But Joseph didn't know what was happening to him.

There was only one thought in his mind: that he was about to die.

A MOOD OF FEAR

In the months leading up to the blazing summer of 1916, a mood of dread had gripped America. People were deeply troubled by news of a war (which would later become known as World War I) that had been raging in Europe for two years. It was a brutal war, pitting England and France and other allied countries against the ruthless forces of Germany and its allies.

Joseph would watch his parents' worried faces as they studied the newspaper each morning, their toast and coffee growing cold as they read about the latest battles. There were horrific descriptions of the fighting—the battlefields soaked in blood, with thousands of soldiers dying in a day.

With each passing week, it was becoming clearer that American forces would have to join the fight to defeat the enemy. Soon millions of US soldiers, many still in their teens, would be crossing the ocean and charging into deadly battles.

What nobody yet knew was that another threat lurked that summer, one far closer to home, in the waters along the New Jersey coast.

During World War I, soldiers spent miserable months in trenches, holes dug into the ground to protect from enemy fire.

The Engleside Hotel, in
Beach Haven, was one of
the fanciest hotels on
the Jersey Shore.

"LOOK OUT!"

The terror had begun eleven days before the attack on Joseph Dunn, on a New Jersey beach seventy-five miles south of Cliffwood. Charles Vansant, a twenty-five-year-old from Philadelphia, was visiting the resort town of Beach Haven. He and his parents and sisters were staying at one of the elegant hotels that lined the beach, and Charles was heading into the ocean for his before-supper swim.

A strong athlete, Vansant loved swimming laps in the ocean. And today he'd made a new friend: a

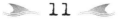

Few Americans knew how to swim in 1916, but wading into the ocean, known as "ocean bathing," was a popular pastime.

large golden retriever that had been playing on the beach. The two set out together in the water, two lone brown heads bobbing above the surf. There were dozens of people on the beach, enjoying the late afternoon breezes before they headed to the hotel dining room for a fine supper.

Vansant and the dog swam out about fifty yards and then, strangely, the dog turned and paddled quickly back toward shore. Vansant called to the dog, but the retriever was already back on the beach, shaking the salty water from its brown fur.

Suddenly, shouts echoed from the beach.

"Look out!"

A few people standing at the shoreline could see what Vansant could not—a large fin knifing through the water.

Vansant must have glimpsed the creature seconds before it attacked. It was a massive shark, eight or nine feet long, its jaws wide open to reveal rows and rows of two-inch-long, razor-sharp teeth. The massive jaws slammed shut around Vansant's left thigh, the teeth tearing through his skin, his muscle, and into his bone.

Vansant's screams rose above the pounding surf, above the chattering couples and laughing children, above the clinking of silverware and glass drifting out from the hotel's dining room. Many people first assumed that Vansant was shouting for the dog to come back into the water.

But Alexander Ott knew that something was

terribly wrong. He was a surfman, a lifeguard patrolling the beach.

Ott sprinted into the water, and in less than a minute, he had reached the young man. Vansant was desperately trying to stay afloat in water stained bright red from his own blood.

Fighting his rising terror, Ott took hold of Vansant's arms. But the shark struck again, once again locking its jaws around Vansant's thigh. This time the shark did not let go.

Five other men rushed in to help.

Mustering all of their strength, they hauled the bleeding young man and the shark attached to his leg into shallower water. The shark's belly was dragging against the sandy bottom when it finally unlocked its jaws and swam away.

The men managed to get Vansant to the beach. He was carried into the hotel lobby and gently laid out on a desk, where a doctor tried desperately to stop his bleeding. His parents and sisters were with him when he died, an hour later.

The dozens of people who witnessed the attack on Charles Vansant had no doubt about what had happened: He had been bitten by a shark. Many had seen the beast with their own eyes—that large dorsal fin poking up through the water, the pointed nose. Alexander Ott had been just feet away from the gigantic fish, close enough to look into its deathly black eyes.

It was, beyond question, a large shark.

But as the story spread, few people believed it.

Yes, Charles Vansant had been attacked by a large sea creature.

But a shark? To most people, that seemed impossible.

Most believed it was a swordfish, whose blade-like nose could easily slice through human flesh. Another possibility was a snapping turtle, a giant

A death certificate for Charles Epting Vansant is shown at top. Partial readable fields include:

FULL NAME OF DECEASED: Charles Epting Vansant

PERSONAL AND STATISTICAL PARTICULARS — MEDICAL CERTIFICATE OF DEATH

male white single

DATE OF DEATH: July 1st 1916

DATE OF BIRTH: August 22 1892

23 - 10

OCCUPATION: student

CAUSE OF DEATH: Hemorrhage from Femoral Artery left side

BIRTHPLACE: Penna

NAME OF FATHER: Eugene L Vansant

Penna

Epting

Beach Haven

SHARK KILLS MAN BATHING IN OCEAN

Physician Dies of Bite Received When Fish Pursues Him at Beach Haven

BEACH HAVEN, July 1.—In view of scores of bathers on the beach, this afternoon, a nine-foot shark followed Dr. E. L. Van Sant in from a swim in the ocean and bit him so badly that he died 30 minutes after being taken to the Engleside Hotel. Cries of warning from the beach as the big man-eater was seen moving swiftly behind the physician came too late. He made frantic efforts to get into safety, but the fish with a mighty dash caught him and the next instant the waves were crimsoned with his blood. Other bathers reached the wounded man and pulled him ashore, but his injuries were such that all efforts to save his life proved unavailing.

DEATH STRUGGLE WITH SHARK DESCRIBED BY ONLOOKERS

Persons on Strand at Beach Haven, N. J., Vainly Tried to Save Man's Life

FURTHER details concerning the tragic death of Charles Epting Vansant became known yesterday, when his body was brought from Beach Haven, N. J., to the home of his father, Dr. E. L. Vansant, at 4038 Spruce street.

Vansant died on Saturday afternoon at the Engleside Hospital, at that seashore resort, after a terrific battle with a nine-foot shark in the surf. He had gone from here with his father and two sisters to spend the week-end there, and on Saturday afternoon was in the surf only a few yards from shore when attacked by the man eater. He was playing with a dog at the time, and onlookers who heard his cries thought them only part of the game.

Vansant tried to get to shore with the jaws of the shark clutching his leg. In the shallow water persons on shore saw the man eater's fin and ran to help him. Led by Alexander Ott, a champion swimmer and a member of the American Olympic team, they drove the shark off and carried its victim to the beach. His leg had been torn from the thigh to the knee. Physicians were called at once, but he died an hour and a half later.

Vansant is well known here, having been graduated from the Episcopal Academy in 1910 and from the University of Pennsylvania in 1914. At the latter institution he was a member of the Glee Club, assistant business manager of the Record, and was on the business staffs of the Punch Bowl and the Red and Blue. At the time of his death he was connected with Folwell Brothers & Co., of this city. He was the only son of Dr. C. L. Vansant, whose offices are at 1829 Chestnut street. His father is a member of the Union League and is a prominent nose and throat specialist.

The funeral will be held from the home here at 11 o'clock on Wednesday morning. The Rev. Dr. Archibald McCallum, of the Walnut Presbyterian Church, will officiate. Interment will be in South Laurel Hill Cemetery.

CHARLES EPTING VANSANT

Above and right: Charles Vansant's gruesome death made headlines. Top: His death certificate states that he was "bitten by shark while bathing." But still, many people refused to believe that he had been attacked by a shark.

reptile armed with jaws powerful enough to snap a human bone in half.

Only a few newspapers reported the incident, and some stories didn't even mention the word *shark*. "Dies after Attack by Fish" was the headline of a short article that appeared in the *New York Times* on July 3.

Why did people have such doubts?

MYSTERIOUS OCEANS

For most Americans in 1916, the oceans covering three-quarters of Earth were as mysterious as distant galaxies. The study of oceans, known as marine biology, was a brand-new science. The ocean's depths were unexplored, a world where mermaids might very well be living in sunken cities, where tentacled sea monsters could be guarding treasure chests overflowing with jewels.

Almost nothing was known about large sharks or any types of sea creatures that weren't routinely

In 1916, scientists
were just beginning
to explore the
ocean's depths.
Here, a man
readies for
a dive in an
early metal
diving
suit.

captured by fishermen or easily observed close to shore.

But there was one "fact" about sharks that most everyone was certain of: No shark would ever bite a live human being. Even the most respected scientists mistakenly believed that sharks were shy creatures with weak jaws and small appetites. Never had there been a proven case of a live person being bitten by a shark. To people living in 1916, the idea that a shark had killed Charles Vansant was as far-fetched as the idea of a deer attacking a man while he was strolling through the woods.

Somehow, news of Vansant's death didn't spread far, and those who'd heard rumors figured it was a freak accident. Americans had enough to worry about with the war in Europe.

A man being killed by a fish wasn't big news.

Until five days later, when it happened again.

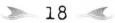

MAN KILLED BY SHARK!

It's unknown whether twenty-seven-year-old Charles Bruder had heard about the tragic death of Charles Vansant. But even if he had, it is unlikely that the story would have stopped him from enjoying his daily swims along the beach in Spring Lake, an elegant vacation town about forty-five miles north of Beach Haven.

Bruder worked at the grand Essex & Sussex Hotel, where his cheerful smile and high spirits made him popular among both the wealthy guests and his fellow workers. When Bruder wasn't hauling trunks and suitcases and helping guests get settled into their rooms, he loved to swim in the ocean until his muscles ached. And that's just what he was doing in the early afternoon of July 6.

He was about 120 yards from shore, his muscular arms churning through the water with graceful strokes. Suddenly, without warning, he was savagely attacked by a large shark.

More than five hundred people were on the beach at the time. Most heard Bruder's screams. One woman glimpsed something red bobbing up and down in the water and was convinced that a red canoe had overturned. She alerted the surfmen, who quickly mobilized for a rescue.

But of course there was no canoe, just the badly injured Bruder struggling to stay afloat in water filled with his own blood. He was near death when the surfmen brought him onto the beach. His injuries were so horrific that men standing on the beach vomited in the sand. Dozens of ladies fainted. Telephone operators were ordered to send warnings to nearby hotels. Within the hour, every beach up and down the shore was closed.

After Bruder died, a respected doctor carefully studied the jagged wounds on his legs and torso. The doctor, also an experienced fisherman, was certain that there was only one marine creature capable of causing such injuries: a large shark. This time, there were few doubts.

By the next morning, headlines blared from the front pages of newspapers around the world.

Monster Shark Kills Again!

Overnight, the image of the shark was transformed. The "tame" creatures of the sea were suddenly seen as bloodthirsty monsters with a taste for human flesh.

As scientists would eventually realize, though, this image of sharks was also incorrect. Large predatory sharks can and do eat just about anything. But today's shark experts agree that even famous "man-eating" species like the great white or the tiger shark do not deliberately seek out humans as prey.

Perhaps the shark that killed Vansant and Bruder was injured or weakened and unable to hunt for its usual prey, such as seals or sea lions.

People dressed modestly in 1916, even while lounging on the beach.

We can never know what caused this shark to attack humans.

But the ferocious man-eater of New Jersey would soon kill again.

A SHARK IN THE CREEK?

By July 12, when Joseph and Michael Dunn and Jerry Hollohan jumped into Matawan Creek, the panic over the shark attacks had died down. The boys must have heard about the attacks, listening to

the grisly stories with pounding hearts and wide-eyed fascination. But why would they worry? Maybe there was a bloodthirsty shark somewhere out in the ocean. But Matawan Creek, fifteen miles inland, seemed as safe as a bathtub.

In fact, the creek was connected to the Atlantic Ocean, its waters rising and falling with the ocean tides. Area fishermen routinely traveled into the creek from the Atlantic. They cut through the Raritan Bay and then drove their boats directly into the creek.

If a boat could make that journey, why couldn't a large shark?

One of the few people who clearly understood this was a retired sea captain named Thomas Cottrell. He had been strolling along the creek earlier that day in the town of Matawan, about one and a half miles from Cliffwood. Gazing out on the water, the old fisherman's eyes locked on a chilling sight—a large fin, slicing through the

mud-brown waters. He stared, dumbstruck, sure his vision was playing tricks on him. But the creature came closer, the sun lighting it up so that Cottrell could have no doubts about what he was looking at: a huge shark.

The captain raced to Main Street and into the crowded barbershop.

"There's a shark in the creek!" he boomed.

Cottrell expected the men to jump to their feet and follow him to the creek.

But nobody budged, and Captain Cottrell couldn't help noticing how some of the men raised their eyebrows and smirked. The captain understood: These people thought he was just a confused old man.

Nobody was going to believe his story.

But the captain had spent years fishing the world's oceans. He had come face-to-face with some of the fiercest beasts in the sea. He was

certain that there was a shark in Matawan Creek, in the same waters where local kids loved to swim.

The captain rushed back to the dock and fired up his motorboat, steering it up the winding creek and shouting out warnings. Joseph, Michael, and Jerry were not yet in the water when the captain was spreading the alarm. And Cottrell just missed another group of swimmers—twelve-year-old Lester Stillwell and his pals, who had come to the creek to cool off. Cottrell's boat was out of sight by the time Lester and his friends arrived at the dock, peeled off their sweaty clothes, and jumped into the water.

What happened next would haunt Lester's friends for the rest of their lives.

Lester was floating on his back when seemingly out of nowhere, the shark exploded out of the water, its enormous jaws wide open. His friends stared in shock as the beast snatched Lester by the arm and pulled him underwater. The boy surfaced just one more time, screaming. But there was nothing for his terrified friends to do but run and get help.

They sprinted into town, half-naked, soaking wet, and sobbing.

"A shark's got Lester!" they cried. "A shark's got Lester!"

The townspeople who saw the hysterical boys knew that something horrific had happened to young Lester Stillwell. Soon, dozens of people were at the dock where the boys had been swimming, shouting out for Lester. It couldn't really be a shark, could it? Was some other monstrous animal in the creek? Had the boy simply drowned?

In the swirl of fear and confusion, one terrible fact could not be denied.

Lester Stillwell was gone.

Two young men at the dock, Stanley Fisher and George Burlow, were determined to at least find Lester's body.

Stanley and George took a rowboat to the middle of the creek and used poles to probe the deep water. When that didn't work, they got into the creek and began to dive to the bottom. Over and over, the men held their breath and dove down, groping blindly in the dark water for Lester's body.

Up and down they went, up and down, as the crowd stood in stunned silence.

And hour passed, then two.

Just when the search seemed hopeless, Fisher burst up through the water, gasping for breath, shouting that he had found Lester's body.

But suddenly, there was a thundering splash.

Fisher's arms flew up in the air.

"He's got me!" he cried.

The shark had clamped its jaws on to Fisher's thigh and was trying to drag him underwater. The crowd stood in helpless horror as Fisher tried to fight off the shark. He pummeled the beast with his fists and tried to gouge it in the eye. He twisted and thrashed. Each time the shark dragged Fisher under the water, Fisher managed to battle his way back up.

And then, miraculously, Fisher broke free from the shark's jaws. Gasping for breath, he managed to swim back to the dock, his face twisted in agony and exhaustion.

Following the deaths of Vansant and Bruder, New Jersey fishermen took to the waters to catch as many sharks as possible.

Men flocked to him, and strong arms hauled Fisher out of the water. When people in the crowd saw Fisher's leg, they erupted in gasps of horror.

Much of Fisher's thigh was gone, the flesh and muscle torn away.

Blood spouted from the gaping wound.

A doctor in the crowd bandaged the leg, and Fisher was whisked away to the hospital.

He would be dead before sunset.

Lester Stillwell's body remained at the bottom of the creek.

SHATTERED AFTERNOON

Meanwhile, only one and a half miles down the creek, Joe, Michael, and Jerry had just started their swim. They had no idea what was happening up the creek.

It wasn't until the shouts of warning shattered their joyful afternoon that they had any idea they were in danger.

And by then, of course, it was too late.

The shark grabbed hold of Joseph Dunn, ready to take its third victim of the day.

But as the shark pulled Joe under the water, Michael and Jerry dove into the creek. They grabbed hold of Joe's arms and tried to wrestle him out of the shark's jaws. It seemed hopeless. The shark was too strong.

But then a sputtering motorboat appeared. It was Captain Cottrell and two other men. Those men jumped into the water to help and were soon part of the terrible match of tug-of-war with the shark. Joseph, numb with shock, was sure he'd be ripped in two. But suddenly, the shark opened its jaws.

Joe was free.

Michael and the men pulled Joe up to the dock and then gently placed him into Captain Cottrell's boat. Joe was alive, although his leg was horribly mangled and bleeding heavily. Michael joined him in the boat and gripped his brother's hand as

In the hours
and days
after the
attacks in
the Matawan
Creek, people
flocked to
the area to
help catch
the killer
shark.

Captain Cottrell gunned the boat back down the creek toward Matawan.

The dock there was still crowded with people. Joe was carried into a motorcar and rushed toward the hospital.

The ten-mile journey to the hospital would take one and a half hours, along a winding, bumpy dirt road.

Nobody believed Joseph Dunn would survive.

The deaths of Charles Bruder and Charles Vansant were horrifying. But the Matawan attacks, in a creek fifteen miles from shore, sent waves of shock around the world. By the next day, America went to war—against sharks. Fishermen charged out to sea, ready to kill any shark on sight. In Matawan, Lester Stillwell's body was finally recovered from the creek. People vowed revenge on the monster that had killed him and Stanley Fisher, both beloved members of their community. Furious men in boats prowled the creek, harpoons raised. Women armed with rifles stood in the tall grass on the creek banks, firing at anything that moved. American president Woodrow Wilson ordered a coast guard ship into the waters off New Jersey with orders to destroy any shark that was spotted.

The shark-killing frenzy would have continued, but on July 14, a man named Michael Schleisser killed a great white shark in Raritan Bay, near Matawan Creek. He hauled the shark to shore and sliced open its stomach. Inside were fifteen pounds of flesh and bones that seemed to belong to a human.

The world rejoiced—the Jersey man-eater had been killed!

There were no more shark attacks that summer, which made it clear to most people that Schleisser had indeed caught the shark that had attacked all five swimmers. Sharks quickly faded out of the headlines as Americans geared up for a far bigger war—World War I. By the following spring, the first American troops were in Europe, fighting the Germans and their allies.

Today, the shark attacks of 1916 have not been forgotten. In fact, many questions remain about what really happened during those twelve days of terror. Was Schleisser's shark really the killer? Was it a great white or a bull shark? Was it one shark or several that committed the attacks? If it was one shark, what caused it to stalk humans with such unnatural ferocity? Scientists continue to study this unusual and horrific event.

One thing is certain, though. For the Dunn family, that summer of 1916 ended on a joyful note.

Joseph Dunn survived his injuries.

On September 15, two months after the attack, he was released from the hospital. He was badly scarred, and limping. But as the months wore on, he fully recovered. He lived into old age, and he

The 7½ ft. Man-Eater and the Man Who Killed It.

Michael Schleisser poses with a seven-and-a-half-foot-long shark he caught off the Jersey Shore. But did he really catch the Jersey man-eater?

hardly ever talked about his experiences of the summer of 1916.

But those who knew Joseph Dunn said he always considered himself a lucky man.

After all, he alone had escaped from the jaws of the New Jersey man-eater.

THE SHARK FILES

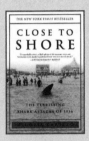

I've been fascinated by the story of the shark attacks of 1916 since 2002, when I read a book called *Close to Shore* by Michael Capuzzo.

About ten years later, I had a chance to revisit the story when I wrote *I Survived the Shark Attacks of 1916*, a historical fiction account of the events.

Like many people, I am endlessly fascinated by sharks, and by our ever-changing ideas about these incredible creatures.

On the following pages, you'll discover more about sharks and what life was like at the time of these shocking events.

IF YOU LIVED IN 1916 . . .

Your name might be . . .

MOST POPULAR
GIRL NAMES:

Mary

Helen

Dorothy

Margaret

Ruth

MOST POPULAR
BOY NAMES:

John

William

James

Robert

Joseph

TINKER TOYS
were introduced
in 1914.

TEDDY BEARS first
became a fad in 1903
and were named after
President Teddy
Roosevelt.

LINCOLN LOGS
were invented
in 1916 and
are still
sold today.

Anne of Green Gables
The Secret Garden
Peter Pan and Wendy
The Wonderful Wizard of Oz

You'd be talking about . . .

THE SINKING OF THE *LUSITANIA*
The elegant British ocean liner
was destroyed by a German
torpedo in 1915.

POLIO
This terrible
disease struck
mostly children,
leaving many paralyzed
and unable to walk
without leg braces.
Today, most kids in the
world are protected
by the polio
vaccine.

THE BABE
Superstar
baseball
player Babe
Ruth was just
starting out his
career with the
Boston Red Sox.

THE ZIPPER
An exciting new
invention!

THE GREAT SHARK DEBATE: WHICH SPECIES WAS THE KILLER OF 1916?

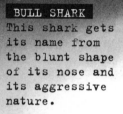

BULL SHARK
This shark gets its name from the blunt shape of its nose and its aggressive nature.

SIZE 7–11.5 feet in length
WEIGHT 200–500 pounds

IT WAS THE BULL SHARK!

Some marine biologists believe that the bull shark is even more aggressive than the great white and responsible for many of the near-shore shark attacks blamed on the great whites.

But the strongest evidence that a bull shark was the 1916 killer is that these sharks have the amazing and unusual ability to survive in brackish water and even freshwater. Bull sharks have even been found in the Mississippi River, hundreds of miles from the ocean.

Scientists don't agree on what kind of shark was behind the shark attacks of 1916. Most agree it was either a great white or a bull shark. Here's how they stack up, so you can weigh in.

GREAT WHITE SHARK
Ancestors of the great white were swimming in the oceans when the *Tyrannosaurus rex* was stomping across the land.

SIZE 15-20 feet in length
WEIGHT 5,000 pounds

IT WAS THE GREAT WHITE SHARK!

Many witnesses to the attacks described a shark with a white belly, which points to a great white. Though great whites cannot survive in freshwater, the water in the creek is brackish, a mix of salt- and freshwater. During high tide, there could have been enough salt water in the creek to enable a great white to survive for a short

SHARKS IN DANGER

Humans are much scarier than sharks.

Every year, about five people die in encounters with sharks . . . and nearly *100 million* sharks are killed by humans. Most sharks are killed for their fins, which are the main ingredient in shark fin soup. This soup is a delicacy prized in many Asian countries.

So many sharks are killed that some species are now endangered. The senseless killing of any creature on Earth is a tragedy. But losing so many big predators like great whites and hammerheads is terrible for our environment as well. That's because these large creatures are very important to keeping ocean ecosystems in balance.

There is some hopeful news, however. Thanks largely to an organization called WildAid, many people in China are refusing to eat shark fin soup. Already, this has cut down on the number of sharks being hunted.

A bowl of shark fin soup can cost more than $100 in some restaurants.

Left: A shark left for dead after its fin was chopped off. Below: Bloody fins hanging on a fishing boat.

Above: Shark fins for sale.

45

SHARK SAFETY

Don't Swim Alone
Sharks are more likely to approach lone swimmers, so always stay in a group.

Don't Swim with a Dog
Dogs' paddling motion resembles the movements of a wounded sea mammal and could attract sharks.

Don't Wear Jewelry
Flashing metal can also attract sharks.

Don't Swim If You're Bleeding
Sharks can detect one drop of blood in an Olympic-size pool.

Avoid Swimming at Dawn or Dusk
This is when sharks feed, so it's best to stay out of the water.

Don't Swim in Vicinity of Seals or Sea Lions
Sea mammals are the favorite prey of big sharks, so steer clear of waters where these creatures are swimming.

Sea mammals like seals and sea lions are favorite meals for large sharks.

DANGER

The motion of a dog swimming is similar to that of an injured seal.

ACCIDENTAL
SHARK ATTACKS?

Scientists don't believe sharks attack people on purpose.

Many shark bites happen when a shark mistakes a swimmer or surfer for a sea mammal, like a seal or sea lion. Others could happen because a shark is curious, and taking a "sample" bite is its way of learning more.

FACT: A person is more likely to be killed by a coconut falling on their head than by a shark.

In October 2003, 13-year-old surfer Bethany Hamilton was bitten by a 14-foot tiger shark. Though she lost an arm, she survived the attack thanks to her friend's father, who slowed the bleeding and rushed her to the hospital. Hamilton soon resumed her surfing career. She also speaks out for the importance of saving sharks in the wild. Her story reveals a truth about shark attacks — most victims survive. In most shark attacks, the shark swims away after just one bite.

Just months after Bethany was injured by a shark, she was back in the water.

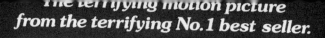

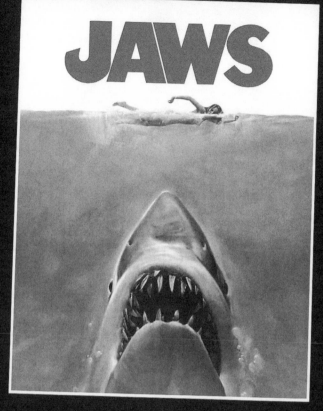

Jaws was a bestselling book and popular movie in the 1970s. But author Peter Benchley regretted that his work made people fear and even hate sharks. He devoted the rest of his life to helping protect sharks.

400 MILLION: Number of years sharks have been swimming in the oceans.

#2

THE VOLCANO THAT CHANGED THE WORLD

THE ERUPTION OF MOUNT TAMBORA, 1815

Ten-year-old John Hoisington stared in shock out the window of his family's Vermont farmhouse. It was June 8, 1816. Summer was just two weeks away. Yet outside, a wild winter snowstorm was raging.

Nearly a foot of snow covered the fields the family had planted only weeks before. The family's vegetable garden was buried. The apple and pear trees shivered in the freezing wind, their delicate buds coated with ice.

Like most people in 1816, the Hoisingtons grew almost everything they ate. Virtually every bite of

the family's food came from the farm, from the corn in their morning porridge to the chicken and potatoes in the suppertime stew. John saw the look of fear in his father's eyes as they watched the snow swirling outside. This storm would kill all of their crops. There would be little food for the family or their horses and cows and other animals.

How would they survive?

What John and his family didn't know was that during that strange summer of 1816, similar weather disasters were unfolding throughout New England—and the world. Snow destroyed thousands of other East Coast farms, from Virginia up to Maine. Snowstorms and floods struck France, England, Ireland, and Switzerland. There were droughts and floods in India and killing frosts across northern China.

At the time, people struggled to understand what had caused the weather to change so wildly. Were witches to blame?

It is only now, two hundred years later, that scientists have finally solved the mystery. Very likely, John Hoisington and his family would have been astonished to learn the truth: The cause of their family's suffering was an event that had taken place a year earlier and ten thousand miles away from their farm.

It all started with a volcano called Mount Tambora.

A RUINED LAND

Mount Tambora sits on the island of Sumbawa, which today is part of the nation of Indonesia. In 1815, perhaps fifty thousand people lived on Sumbawa, a beautiful land of rushing streams, gentle hills, and thick jungles. Looming over the northern side of the island was Mount Tambora, a quiet mountain dotted with villages and rice farms. Nobody had any reason to suspect that the peaceful mountain was in fact a volcano, that underneath its velvety green slopes were snaking tunnels filled with magma and explosive gases. Like many volcanoes, Tambora looked like an ordinary mountain and had been dormant—quiet—for centuries. But on April 5, 1815, Tambora woke up.

The first eruption shook the island and sent up great plumes of fire and ash. But that was nothing compared with what would come five days later, on April 10.

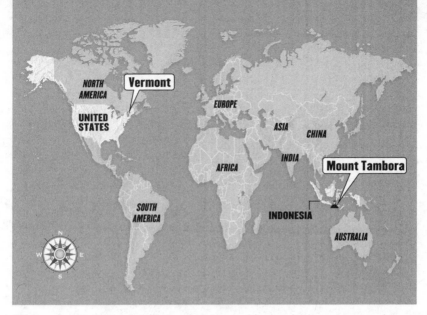

This map, showing the world as it is today, can give
you a sense of the great distances that the ash
cloud from Tambora spread. Thousands of miles away
in Vermont and other New England states, farmers
like the Hoisingtons were ruined as the ash cloud
lowered temperatures and triggered extreme weather.

KABOOM!

The volcano exploded with terrible fury, spewing
out great towers of fire. A tremendous cloud of gas
and ash shot high into the sky. The day turned
midnight-black, but the mountain glowed red as
rivers of lava gushed down the slopes. The eruption

The people of Sumbawa
had no way of escaping
the lava, ash, and
poisonous gases
that spewed from
Mount Tambora. Many
were killed in the
explosion. Thousands
more died of starvation
in the months after.

went on for more than three days, a deadly storm of fire, gas, ash, and rock. In the eruption's terrifying final stage, a wave of flames and gases swept down the mountain at speeds of 400 miles per hour. This pyroclastic surge devastated everything in its path.

IGNORED AND FORGOTTEN

The eruption instantly killed at least twelve thousand people living on and around Mount Tambora. Ash and lava ruined the island's soil and poisoned its rivers and streams. Rice paddies were destroyed. No fruits or vegetables would grow. There were no fish to catch, and almost every animal had been killed. Trapped without food on their ruined lands, more than ninety thousand people on Sumbawa and the nearby island of Lombok slowly starved to death.

The eruption of Tambora in 1815 was the most deadly and powerful volcanic eruption on Earth in the past ten thousand years. Its explosive energy was ten times stronger than that of Krakatoa, history's most famous volcano. Krakatoa erupted in 1883, also in the island chain now known as Indonesia.

And yet, incredibly, few people outside the blast zone learned about this terrible disaster. The people of Sumbawa and surrounding islands led simple lives. Few of them had any connections to far-off lands like Europe or the Americas. Some British sailors witnessed the eruption. But news and information traveled very slowly in 1815. The only way to get a letter (or a person) across oceans was on a sailing ship. The voyage from Sumbawa to New York or London would have taken perhaps four months. Eventually, reports of the eruption did make it back to England, but few people paid attention. Somehow, the deadliest volcano in history was ignored by most of the world—and then forgotten.

What people *were* paying attention to a year

Summer snowstorms destroyed crops in New England.

later, in 1816, was the terrible weather—snowstorms in the summer, floods that turned wheat fields into lakes, frosts that blackened millions of acres of farmland around the world. Farmers up and down the East Coast lost their crops. In Europe, farmers grew desperate. In Paris, mobs of people broke into warehouses where grain was stored, risking their lives to steal sacks of flour. In China, starving families could no longer feed their children. Floods in India triggered an outbreak of a disease called cholera, which killed millions.

SOLVING A MYSTERY

In 1816, not even the most brilliant scientists would have believed that these weather problems were somehow connected—that all these disasters had been caused by the eruption of a volcano few had heard of. Little was known about climate or volcanoes. But today, scientists know that volcanoes can have a major impact on weather worldwide. They have learned by studying recent volcanic eruptions, like that of Mount Pinatubo in the Philippines.

Scientists monitored every phase of Pinatubo's eruption in June 1991. It was not as powerful as Tambora's. But the eruption was monstrous, one of the most powerful since Krakatoa, and the second-largest of the twentieth century.

Using satellites and computers, scientists tracked the volcano's huge eruption cloud as it rose into the

The Eruption of
Mount Pinatubo,
Philippines,
June 1991

▲ A truck speeds
away from Pinatubo's
massive ash cloud.

▲ Villages surrounding
Pinatubo were buried
in ash and mud.

sky. Most volcanic clouds quickly dissipate—break apart and fade away. But in a very powerful eruption, the cloud rises so high that it mixes with water vapor and other gases in the stratosphere. It turns into a foam and remains high in the sky. Scientists observed Pinatubo's cloud as it spread across the world. Like a layer of sunscreen slathered across the sky, the cloud blocked out some of the sun's heat and light. Temperatures dropped, and storms became more violent. It took three years for Pinatubo's foamy haze to clear. Tambora's cloud

▲ Scientists flocked to the
Philippines to study the area
in Pinatubo's blast zone.

would have been even bigger, its effects more
devastating. Indeed, like an invisible beast,
Tambora's cloud hovered in the sky for about three
years. By the time the climate returned to normal,
as many as thirty million people had died from
Tambora's effects. And many more lives—like the
Hoisingtons'—had been forever changed.

John and his family survived the loss of their
crops. But they gave up their farm and moved west
to Ohio. They started their trek in June 1817,
traveling in an oxcart piled with their possessions.

Tens of thousands of other New England farmers made similar journeys, many driven west by the hardships of 1816. It was one of the biggest migrations in US history. Most migrants went to Ohio, Indiana, and Illinois. Farmland in this fresh wilderness was cheap, and the soil was much easier to farm than in rocky New England.

The Hoisingtons' thousand-mile journey took three months. John's older sister, Sabrina, recorded the trip in her diary. She described the family's meeting with Native Americans, long days of slogging through mud, and some enjoyable

The weather disaster triggered by Tambora caused thousands of people from Connecticut, Vermont, and other New England states to abandon their farms. Many headed west.

66

visits with friends they met along the way. They arrived in Ohio in August and were soon settled in to life on their new farm.

Meanwhile, ten thousand miles away, the volcano that had nearly destroyed their lives went back to sleep, sitting in silence to this day—until it wakes again.

THE VOLCANO FILES

While researching *I Survived the Destruction of Pompeii*, I was shocked to discover that the deadliest volcanic eruption in recorded history was Mount Tambora, which I had never heard of. I learned so much, including the facts that follow.

Colombia's Nevado del Ruiz volcano had the fourth-deadliest volcanic eruption in recorded history.

IF YOU LIVED IN 1815 . . .

You worked HARD.

There wasn't much free time for American kids in 1815. Most likely you lived on a small farm. You woke up before dawn to milk cows and feed chickens before school. During planting and harvest season, school was canceled so you could work all day.

You might have been a slave.

In fact, if you were African American and living in the South, you were almost certainly enslaved. This meant that everything about your life was controlled by the person who owned you. By 1820, 1.5 million men, women, and children were enslaved in the United States.

Your school was one room.

In one-room schoolhouses, kindergartners sat alongside high schoolers and were all taught by one teacher, usually a very young woman. Many teachers were still in their teens.

Most kids learned to read using this book, known as the *Blue Back Speller*.

A BLOODY WAR ENDS

One reason few Americans heard about the eruption of
Mount Tambora was that they were distracted by a bloody
war: the War of 1812.

This war isn't as well known as the Revolutionary War or
the Civil War. But it should be. Thousands of US soldiers were
killed in terrible battles. British troops burned down most of
Washington, DC, including the White House.

The war raged for three years and ended in a tie. But it was
a win for the young United States. America had taken on the
most powerful country in the world—Great Britain. And had
come out strong.

"The Star-Spangled Banner" Is Born

The War of 1812 is perhaps best known for the poem it inspired, "Defence of Fort M'Henry." Francis Scott Key wrote it during the Battle of Baltimore. The poem later became our national anthem, with a new name, "The Star-Spangled Banner."

History's Deadliest Volcanoes

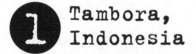

1 Tambora, Indonesia

YEAR: 1815   **DEATHS:** 92,000
MAIN CAUSE OF DEATHS: starvation

Krakatoa, Indonesia

YEAR: 1883   **DEATHS:** 32,000
MAIN CAUSE OF DEATHS: tsunami

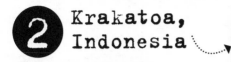 **Mount Pelée, Martinique (Caribbean)**

YEAR: 1902   **DEATHS:** 29,024
MAIN CAUSE OF DEATHS: flows of ash

 Nevado del Ruiz, Colombia

YEAR: 1985   **DEATHS:** 25,000
MAIN CAUSE OF DEATHS: mudslides

1,500:
The number of active volcanoes in the world today.

 Unzen, Japan

YEAR: 1792   **DEATHS:** 14,300
MAIN CAUSE OF DEATHS: collapse of volcano

Giant Volcano in Space

The tallest volcano in the solar system is on Mars. Olympus Mons is 15.5 miles high. This is more than twice as tall as Earth's biggest volcano, Mauna Kea, in Hawaii.

Yellowstone
National Park:

SUPERVOLCANO

Deep under the surface of one of the world's most beautiful parks is one of the largest volcanoes on Earth.

Two million years ago, a massive eruption blasted away mountain peaks and left a flattened land of geysers, hot springs, and exotic lakes.

This "supervolcano" is still active, and another explosion is likely. Will it be a major disaster? Such a blast could blanket much of the western United States in ash and impact our climate for years. Little wonder that volcano scientists are keeping a close watch on Yellowstone.

Lava Explorers

There is no stopping a volcanic eruption from happening, but scientists around the world are working hard to monitor dangerous volcanoes. The goal is to give people plenty of warning and time to evacuate before an eruption.

MY RESEARCH JOURNEY

My information came from many sources, but here are some highlights!

THE SPARK

I first discovered the story of Tambora in a review of a book called *The Year Without Summer*. I read the book and was hooked!

LEARNING MORE

I read another amazing book, *Tambora: The Eruption That Changed the World*. This taught me even more about Tambora and its effects.

FINDING JOHN

I wanted to build my story around a New England family. My *Storyworks* colleague Allison Friedman worked with the Vermont Historical Society to find the diary of Sabrina Hoisington.

#3

THE BLOODRED NIGHT

THE GREAT PESHTIGO FIRE OF 1871

On Sunday morning, October 8, 1871, seven-year-old John Kramer could not have imagined that he was about to come face-to-face with the deadliest fire in American history. By the end of the night, though, his town of Peshtigo, Wisconsin, would be burned to ashes. As many as 2,500 people would be dead.

It had been a difficult but exciting year for the Kramer family: John; his parents, Joseph and Katherine; and his nine-year-old brother, Mike. They had come to the United States from Germany more than a decade earlier. They had settled first in the rolling farmland of upstate New York. In 1870, they decided to head west for the young state of Wisconsin. Thousands of new immigrants had made the same westward journey, lured by the promise of cheap farmland and the chance to carve a brand-new life out of the fresh American wilderness.

And what a wilderness it was!

Most of Wisconsin at that time was covered with forests—billions and billions of trees growing on thousands of square miles of land. These were the forests of fairy tales and elves, with towering trees, howling wolves, and dagger-clawed bears. One early Wisconsin settler was Laura Ingalls Wilder, author of the Little House series. She was born in a north-woods cabin just three years before the Kramers arrived in the area. "The great, dark trees of the Big Woods stood all around the house," she wrote. "And beyond them were other trees, and beyond them were more trees. As far as a man

There are no forests left on Earth as large as those that covered Wisconsin and Minnesota until the late 1800s. Today, a few patches of preserved forest lands capture the beauty of what has been lost.

could go to the north in a day, or a week, or a whole month, there was nothing but woods."

Laura wasn't exaggerating.

The forest that stretched across northern Wisconsin and into Minnesota was like no other on Earth. For centuries, those woods were mostly undisturbed by humans. Native Americans hunted and fished among the towering trees. The only sounds to be heard were the chirps of birds, the growls of wild animals, and the soft whisper of leaves rustling in the wind.

By the time John and his family arrived, though, big changes were happening in Wisconsin's woods.

CHOP, CHOP, CHOP

American cities were booming in the second half of the 1800s, especially Chicago, 250 miles south of Peshtigo. Just forty years earlier, Chicago had been a small city on a mosquito-ridden marsh. By 1871, it was the fastest-growing city in the world. Every day, new buildings were rising—mansions and shops, warehouses and department stores. Chicago builders needed a seemingly endless supply of wood for all this construction, and they found it in the great forests of northern Wisconsin.

Beginning in the 1860s, lumber companies bought up huge chunks of the northern woods.

Above: Logs were transported by river, but sometimes thousands of logs became stuck in "logjams." The men sent to clear these jams risked being crushed.
Below: A cart filled with cut Wisconsin trees.

They sent out armies of lumberjacks to chop down trees. The trees were then stripped of their branches, dragged by oxcart across the forest, and dumped into the Peshtigo River. The river's rushing waters carried the giant logs downstream to Peshtigo's sawmill, where they were transformed into lumber for building.

By 1870, the forest surrounding Peshtigo echoed with the curses and shouts of lumberjacks, the chop, chop, chop of axes, and the thundering crashes of 150-foot-tall trees hitting the ground. Once an area of forest had been stripped, lumber companies were happy to sell the land to farmers like John's parents.

Right away, the Kramers felt at home in Wisconsin, where they met many fellow German immigrants. Within a year, they had finished building their house. The boys were thriving, and everything looked hopeful.

Then came the fire.

A CHOKING FOG

As the Kramers quickly learned, fires were a fact of life in the northern woods. Though some fires were sparked by lightning, most were set intentionally. Lumberjacks lit fires to destroy the branches they hacked off the trees. Farmers used fire to clear their land of tree stumps and brush left behind by the lumberjacks. At times, there were so many fires burning that a choking fog of smoke hung over Peshtigo.

The early fall of 1871 had been a particularly bad time for fires. Little rain had fallen during the summer, and the entire Midwest of the United States was parched. Creeks had dried up. Trees had withered. On September 24, a series of fires began to burn out of control in and around Peshtigo. The blazes burned hundreds of acres of forestland and destroyed homes and shops in nearby communities. The town's biggest factory caught fire. Hundreds of men rushed to fight the flames with buckets of water from the river. They managed to save the building, but dozens of men were injured in the exhausting battle.

That fire cast a spell of fear over Peshtigo. Some people were so spooked that they packed up and left the area for good. But the Kramers had spent every penny they had on their move to Peshtigo. They had worked day and night to clear their land and build their house. They didn't have the money—or the heart—to simply abandon their land and start again someplace new. And neither did most of their neighbors.

All they could do was try to prepare. Many people buried their most treasured possessions deep in the dirt. Farmers kept soaking-wet blankets in their barns to protect their animals from airborne sparks. Many kept their horses hitched to wagons in case they needed to make a quick escape. The Kramers cleared their land of every speck of dried brush and wood.

But as it would turn out, there was no way to prepare for the horror that was to come.

A BLOODRED SKY

October 8 dawned unnaturally hot, and the sky glowed orange from the many small fires smoldering in the forest. John's parents could see flames lapping at the edge of the forest, and they sensed disaster was coming soon. They were determined to save their home. But they wanted the boys out of the fire's reach.

There was a forty-acre field on a neighbor's farm, freshly plowed and free of any trees or brush that could burn. Mrs. Kramer gave the boys strict instructions to go to the middle of the field and wait there until she or their father fetched them. Doom must have filled John's heart as he and his brother, Mike, headed toward the field. Would they ever see their parents again?

As the day wore on, the smoke thickened, and

the sky turned bloodred. Strong winds swept into the region. Many hoped that a soaking rainstorm was on the way, and that soon the risk of fire would pass.

But there would be no rain that night, only winds—violent, swirling gusts. Whipped up by the wind, the small fires in the forest grew bigger until, finally, they all joined together into one monstrous inferno. Flames towered hundreds of feet into the sky. Trees exploded from the extreme heat. Flaming hunks of wood flew across the forest, setting fires miles away.

Father Peter Pernin, a Peshtigo priest, wrote a detailed account of his experiences in the fire, which was later published as a book.

Around 10:00 P.M., the people of Peshtigo heard an earsplitting roar, which Father Peter Pernin later compared to the sound of a speeding freight train.

No photographers captured the Peshtigo fire, but in the weeks following, newspaper artists re-created the events for people around the world.

In fact, it was the sound of a fire erupting from the forest, a blaze of extraordinary size, power, and heat. The fire was no longer simply a fire, but a firestorm. These rare fires happen when there are strong winds and large amounts of flammable material—like trees—to feed the flames. Firestorms burn far hotter than regular fires and create their own swirling winds and explosive gases.

For most people nearby, the sound of the fire blasting out of the forest would be the last sound they would ever hear.

SHEETS OF FLAME

John's parents fled their home moments before the explosion. They knew their house would be destroyed. Now they just wanted to find the boys. They left with only one possession—a mattress stuffed with feathers—and started toward the plowed field where they had sent the boys.

But John's parents would never make it to the field.

The wall of fire now stretched thousands of feet across and rose high into the sky. It was moving faster than even the most modern trains of 1871. Escape was impossible.

Right: A modern artist brings to life the terrifying scene in Peshtigo, where not even the river provided safety for fleeing victims.

A rare photo showing the aftermath of the Peshtigo fire. The railroad tracks are littered with the remains of trains that were burned.

All seemed hopeless for John's parents, until they noticed a well dug deep into the ground. First, they soaked their mattress with water from the well.

Then they climbed into the well, pulling the mattress on top of themselves.

As the Kramers hid inside the well, clinging to each other in terror, they could not begin to imagine the scene of horror unfolding all around Peshtigo. The heat and the flames killed hundreds of people instantly. Others died trying to flee to the river. The Kramers could hear the fire roaring above them. They did not expect to survive the night.

And neither did John and Mike, who huddled together in the middle of the plowed field, burying their faces in the loose dirt to protect themselves from the unbearable heat.

The fire raged for hours. It leveled the town of Peshtigo and sixteen other towns to the north. By morning, more than a billion trees were gone, and an area twice the size of Rhode Island was a sea of charred trees and ash.

Nobody knows how many people died, though most agree it was between 1,000 and 2,500.

THE MOST DEADLY FIRE

Miraculously, all of the Kramers survived.

John and Mike staggered out of the field, their eyes seared by the thick smoke, their clothes covered with ash. Joseph and Katherine climbed out of the well, shivering and in shock but untouched by the flames.

As John would say decades later, the joy of their reunion carried the Kramer family through the many difficult months ahead.

In an incredible twist of events, another cata-strophic fire had happened the very same night as the one that destroyed Peshtigo—the Great Chicago Fire. The same drought and fierce winds that drove the flames through the Wisconsin forests leveled much of Chicago. Some eighteen thousand build-ings were destroyed, and approximately three hundred people were killed.

Chicago's fire made news around the world. Aid poured in from neighboring states. Even

Wisconsin's governor, Lucius Fairchild, rushed to Chicago to assist in the relief efforts.

Meanwhile, Peshtigo was cut off from the world. Its telegraph lines and railroads had been destroyed. It was days before news of the Peshtigo disaster even reached Wisconsin's capital, Madison. With Governor Fairchild in Chicago, it was up to the governor's wife, Frances, to organize rescue efforts to Peshtigo.

Even after help arrived, life in Peshtigo was bleak. The town was gone, as were most of the people. Many survivors left, hoping to put the horrifying memories behind them.

But the Kramers decided to stay and help rebuild. John eventually married and had six children. He was still living in Peshtigo when he died at the age of eighty-one, surrounded by his children and four grandchildren.

History has largely forgotten the Great Peshtigo Fire. But John's grandchildren will always know that their lucky grandfather miraculously survived the most deadly fire in US history.

WISCONSIN
OFFICIAL MARKER

PESHTIGO FIRE CEMETERY

On the night of October 8, 1871, Peshtigo, a booming town of 1700 people, was wiped out of existence in the greatest forest fire disaster in American history.

Loss of life and even property in the great fire occurring the same night in Chicago did not match the death toll and destruction visited upon northeastern Wisconsin during the same dreadful hours.

The town of Peshtigo was centered around a woodenware factory, the largest in the country. Every building in the community was lost. The tornado of fire claimed at least 800 lives in this area. Many of the victims lie here. The memory of 350 unidentified men, women, and children is preserved in a nearby mass grave.

Erected in 1951 by the people of Peshtigo.

THE PESHTIGO FIRE FILES

I learned about the Peshtigo fire while I was working on *I Survived the Great Chicago Fire, 1871*. What a shock it was to learn that this fire, the deadliest in US history, blazed on the *very same night* as the Great Chicago Fire. Turn the page to learn more about Peshtigo and other intriguing facts I uncovered in my research.

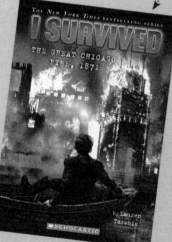

I get many story ideas while researching my I Survived books.

AMERICA IN 1871

A COUNTRY ON THE MOVE

America was growing fast, with thirty-seven states.
Thanks to the new transcontinental railroad,
finished in 1869, you could travel from coast to
coast in record time (about seven days).

CIVIL WAR GHOSTS

In 1871, Americans were still recovering
from the Civil War, the bloody war
between the states of the North and the
states of the South. The North won,
and slavery became illegal. But 750,000
soldiers died, and many more suffered
terrible and lasting injuries.

104

FROM SLAVERY TO FREEDOM

Slavery had ended, but most African Americans lived in poverty, especially in the South. There weren't nearly enough schools for all of the former slaves who wanted an education.

NATIVE AMERICAN TRAGEDY

As American settlers moved west, hundreds of thousands of Native Americans were forced off their lands. By 1871, most were living on grim reservations, and their way of life was coming to an end.

LEARNING FROM FIRE

Three of America's deadliest fires have taught us important lessons that make us safer today.

1 The Great Chicago Fire, 1871

Then

The Chicago fire shocked the world, but fire experts had been warning for years that the city, built mainly of wood, was likely to burn. The following year, laws were passed requiring public buildings to be made from fire-resistant materials such as brick and stone.

Now

2 The Iroquois Theater Fire, 1903

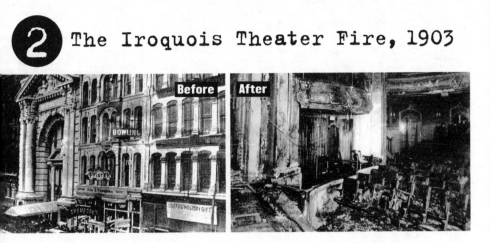
Before / After

Twenty-five years after the Great Chicago Fire, a far deadlier blaze broke out in Chicago, at its most elegant theater. More than 600 people died. The tragedy brought about stricter fire safety laws for public buildings, including requirements for improved fire exits, fireproof scenery, and sprinkler systems above the stage.

3 The Cocoanut Grove Fire, 1942

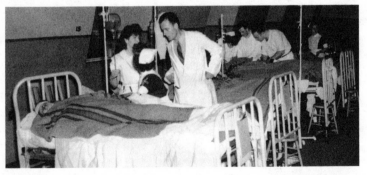

A deadly fire at a packed Boston nightclub killed 492 people and injured hundreds more. Many of the injured were saved using brand-new treatments for burns; survival rates were far higher than in previous fires.

FACTS
ABOUT WILDFIRES

EVERY YEAR,
there are an average of
70,000
wildfires in the
United States.

In 2012,
9.33 million acres were
destroyed
by wildfires.
That area is larger than
Connecticut, Delaware, and
Rhode Island combined.

Lightning

causes 10 percent
of all wildfires.

About 90 percent
of wildfires are
caused by

humans.

Campfires, sparks
caused by machinery,
and cigarette smoking
are most to blame.

Wildfires move at

14 miles
per hour

(about as fast as you
can ride your bike).

REAL-LIFE
SUPERHEROES

When wildfires threaten wilderness areas, smoke jumpers come to the rescue.

RESCUE FROM THE SKY

Smoke jumpers are firefighters specially trained to battle fires in wilderness areas. They often reach a fire by parachute.

STOPPING THE FIRE'S SPREAD

By clearing away brush and dried grass, smoke jumpers deprive the fire of the fuel it needs to spread. These cleared areas are known as firebreaks.

EMERGENCY SHELTERS

American smoke jumpers carry emergency fire shelters, fire-resistent cocoons they can climb inside if they are trapped by a fire. Since 1977, these shelters have saved about 300 lives and prevented serious burns for many more.

THE MOST DANGEROUS JOB

In 2013, nineteen firefighters known as the Granite Mountain Hotshots lost their lives in an Arizona wildfire. Most were in their fire shelters when they were overtaken by smoke and flames. This shows that even with modern safety equipment, fighting wildfires is one of the most dangerous jobs in the world.

FIGHTING FIRES
YESTERDAY AND

Horse Power

At the time of the Peshtigo fire, firefighters relied on horse-drawn hose carts and steam-powered pumpers. These could not be brought into a forest.

Bucket Brigades

Many small towns didn't even have firefighting equipment. They relied on bucket brigades. People would line up between a river or pump and the fire, passing buckets of water. Not surprisingly, large fires were often impossible to fight.

TODAY

Now

Air Support

Firefighters on the ground get support from air tankers and helicopters. Aircraft can drop thousands of gallons of water on a fire. Planes also drop fire retardants, chemicals that slow and cool the fire. A large plane can drop 11,900 gallons of fire retardant at one time.

EVER HEARD OF SMOKEY THE BEAR?

In 1950, a tiny bear cub barely survived a raging wildfire in New Mexico's Capitan Mountains. The cub was rescued and named Smokey. He was eventually sent to the National Zoo in Washington, DC, where he became a mascot for preventing wildfires.

REMEMBER! only you can PREVENT FOREST FIRES

YOUR FIRE SAFETY CHECKLIST

These steps can help keep you and your family safe.

 PRACTICE AT HOME You should have fire drills at home just like at school. You and your family should practice how you would escape from your house in case of a fire.

 PICK A MEETING PLACE Choose a safe spot near your house where you and your family can meet in case you all escape separately.

 GET OUT RIGHT AWAY Don't try to collect your treasures. Just get out as quickly as you can.

 DON'T COOK ALONE Want to make dinner for your family? Great, but make sure an adult is right there in the kitchen with you.

For more information, go to **Sparky.org**.

#4

THE INVISIBLE MONSTER

ONE GIRL'S ENCOUNTER WITH
THE DEADLY BOX JELLYFISH

The year was 2009 and it was a bright day in December, which is summer in Australia. Ten-year-old Rachael Shardlow and her brother, Sam, age thirteen, were swimming in one of their favorite spots on the Calliope River in Queensland. This swimming area is about fifteen miles from where the river empties into the Pacific Ocean.

Rachael was floating in the cool, clean water, practicing her flips.

Suddenly, she felt a burning pain on her legs. At first, she felt as though she had been sliced by something sharp. But within seconds, it seemed that her legs and one arm were on fire. She looked down and saw, to her horror, that she was entangled with an enormous jellyfish. Its large head was square, and its tentacles seemed to stretch endlessly into the water. Several of the tentacles, each no thicker than a strand of spaghetti, were wrapped around Rachael's legs and arms.

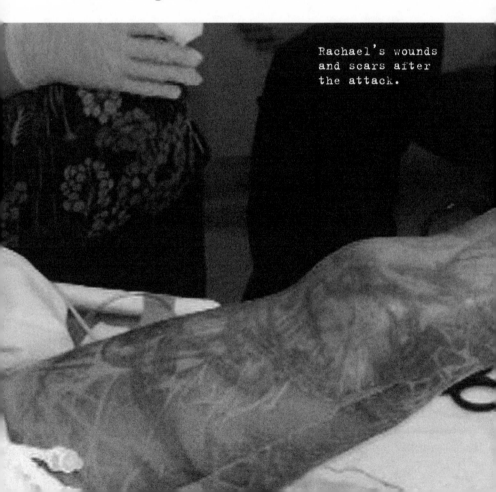

Rachael's wounds and scars after the attack.

Rachael had no idea that she was now in the grip of one of the world's deadliest creatures—*Chironex fleckeri*, better known as the box jellyfish. Each of the tentacles is armed with half a million microscopic harpoons called nematocysts, which are loaded with powerful venom. The moment the tentacles made contact with Rachael's body, thousands of

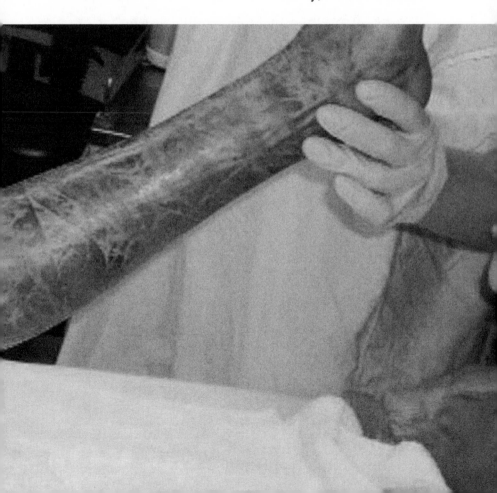

those tiny harpoons were fired into her skin, each injecting her with deadly venom.

Her skin burned. Her heart felt as though it was being squeezed in her chest. Rachael's brother heard her screams and ran through the water to help her. One of the jellyfish's tentacles brushed his leg, searing him. In spite of his pain, Sam dragged his sister to shore and shouted for help.

"I can't see!" Rachael whispered to her brother. "I can't breathe."

Moments later, as her parents rushed over, Rachael fell unconscious. The terrifying creature was still wrapped around her legs and one of her arms.

HORROR-MOVIE CREATURE

Australia is home to some of the world's most-feared creatures. There's the eastern brown snake—lightning fast, furiously aggressive, and the second-most-venomous snake in the world. There's the Sydney funnel-web spider—more toxic than

Australia is famous for its variety of deadly creatures, including the eastern brown snake and the funnel-web spider.

any other and prone to nesting in sock drawers and toy chests. And, of course, there is the ferocious great white shark, which lurks in large numbers in the waters off Australia's south coast.

But no venomous creature in Australia—or on Earth—compares with the box jellyfish, which is also known as the marine stinger or sea wasp.

It certainly looks terrifying, more like an alien from a horror movie than a creature we would expect to meet during an afternoon swim. Its head is enormous, resembling a squared-off basketball.

It has twenty-four unblinking eyes and clusters of tentacles that can grow to be nine feet long. Its venom is a deadly mixture of chemicals that can kill a large man in three minutes.

Nobody knows how many of these dangerous creatures dwell along the coast of northern Australia. They have also been found off the coasts of Vietnam and the Philippines. Over the decades, it

Many beaches in Australia are routinely closed due to the risk of box jellyfish stings.

is estimated that as many as 100 people have died from their stings. So dangerous are these jellyfish that for seven months out of every year, from October through April, some of northern Australia's most beautiful beaches must be closed to swimmers. Box jellyfish are virtually invisible in the water: Imagine a shredded plastic bag floating quietly by. This makes them almost impossible for swimmers to avoid.

They prefer shallow waters close to shore and often head into estuaries, saltwater areas where rivers and ocean meet. Everywhere you travel along the coast, marine stinger warning signs appear. Rescue stations at most campgrounds and beaches stock jugs of vinegar, which has long been believed to help neutralize the venom of all jellyfish.

STILL NOT BREATHING

No warning signs were posted around the swimming area where Rachael and Sam were playing that day. That's because it is unusual for a box jellyfish to travel so far up the river, away from the ocean. There was no vinegar, either. But two of the people who responded to Sam's screams for help that day were experienced coastal campers. Knowing they would be at remote beaches, they had brought vinegar along with them. They retrieved

Bottles of vinegar are provided in areas where box jellyfish are common. However, recent studies question whether this old remedy is actually helpful or harmful.

MARINE STINGERS
ARE PRESENT
IN THESE WATERS
DURI**
SUMM**

✚ VINEGAR
For use on MARINE STINGS
POUR ON - DO NOT RUB
SEEK MEDICAL ATTE NTION

it from their tent and doused Rachael's legs and arms. The jellyfish fell from her body, but Rachael remained unconscious. Her heart had stopped beating.

Her father lifted her up and ran with her in his arms to their car. As her mother drove, her father administered CPR. For eight minutes, he pushed on Rachael's chest and breathed air into her lungs. She still was not breathing when they reached paramedics in town, who sped her to the hospital.

No person had ever survived such a severe box jellyfish sting.

UNLOCKING MYSTERIES

News of Rachael's tragic situation quickly spread across Australia. The news reports soon caught the attention of Dr. Jamie Seymour, a venom biologist at James Cook University in the nearby city of Cairns. For years, Seymour has been trying to unlock mysteries that will help Australians avoid such dangerous encounters. So intense is his interest in Australia's venomous jellyfish that he has earned the nickname the Jelly Dude from Nemo Land.

But don't let that nickname fool you.

Seymour is dead serious about venomous creatures and has dedicated his career to unlocking their secrets.

On any given day, you might find Seymour in waist-deep water, staring down as though he has lost a contact lens. What he's really doing is looking for box jellyfish. Or, more specifically, he is looking for the shadows the creatures cast on the ocean floor. This is the only way to spot their transparent bodies in the water. When he sees one, he scoops it into a bin and goes to work.

Left: Dr. Jamie Seymour, wearing protective gloves, handles box jellyfish in his lab and the ocean. Above: A marine biologist gets an up-close look.

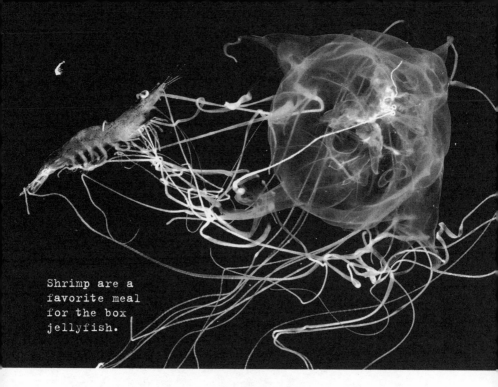

Shrimp are a
favorite meal
for the box
jellyfish.

Using special glue (and wearing a thick suit
and gloves of protective rubber), he attaches a
transmitter to one of its tentacles. He then releases
it back into the water. The transmitter allows
Seymour to track the jellyfish until the glue wears
off, usually in a few days. Over the years, Seymour
has been able to gather some intriguing information
about how this creature behaves.

For example, scientists always believed that box jellyfish were little more than giant blobs of slime floating aimlessly around the ocean. But as Seymour discovered, a box jellyfish isn't so simple after all. The creatures seem to sleep at night. They sink to the bottom of the ocean, close their twenty-four eyes, and snooze. This enables them to hide from their main predator, a kind of sea turtle that hunts at night. The turtle's skin is so thick and leathery that it is not affected by the box jellyfish's venom.

Another surprise: The jellyfish don't just drift along in the current. These creatures are actually propelling themselves along at speeds of about five miles an hour. (That's about as fast as you can walk.)

But Seymour's most shocking discovery is that these creatures aren't just mindless blobs. They move with purpose. Those two dozen eyes enable it to track its favorite prey, shrimp and small fish. Though the box jellyfish doesn't have an actual brain, Seymour discovered that it somehow processes information. In other words, a box jellyfish knows what it's doing.

RED-HOT KNIFE

When Seymour heard about Rachael Shardlow's injuries, his thoughts were grim. He himself has suffered from minor stings. "Imagine someone slicing your skin with a red-hot knife, then magnify that pain by one hundred," he has said. "Then hold on to that pain for twenty minutes."

But the venom doesn't just cause pain. The chemicals have a powerful and devastating effect on different parts of the human body, including the heart and the brain. Seymour didn't believe that Rachael could survive such a serious sting.

He was happy to be wrong.

Doctors were able to restart Rachael's heart and get her breathing on her own.

Rachael was in the hospital for several weeks. She suffered from some mild memory problems for

The box jellyfish is almost invisible in the water.

the first few months she was home. Her scars will be permanent, but she has fully recovered. Warning signs are now posted along the Calliope River.

Dr. Seymour continues his work, hunting those deadly shadows. In April 2014, he publicized new findings about how to treat box jellyfish stings. His research showed that vinegar could actually be harmful. He discovered that vinegar could cause those tiny harpoons in the box jellyfish's tentacles—the nematocysts—to inject even more venom into a victim. The key to surviving a box jellyfish attack, Seymour says, is performing CPR to keep the victim alive until doctors can take over. What saved Rachael's life was likely Rachael's father, who knew CPR.

Then

Rachael rests a few weeks after the box jellyfish attack.

Seymour hopes that further breakthroughs are in the future. His goal, he says, is that one day, Australians will be able to swim without fear.

Surely, Rachael shares that hope.

Now

THE JELLYFISH FILES

The box jellyfish is just one of many species that inspire fear and fascination. Turn the page to learn more about jellyfish and to come face-to-face with other intriguing and deadly creatures.

Beware of beautiful frogs, dancing scorpions, and swaying cobras!

FACTS
ABOUT JELLYFISH

Jellyfish have
no brains.

Jellyfish are
not actually fish.

There are more than
2,000
species of jellyfish.

The largest jellyfish, the LION'S MANE, can grow to be more than
7 feet
in diameter.

Jellyfish are found in
every ocean
on the planet.

Jellyfish are about **95%** water.

Jellyfish populations are **growing fast** around the world.

Some jellyfish **glow** in the dark.

In many parts of the world, the word for jellyfish is **medusa**, inspired by the snake-haired creature from Greek mythology.

AUSTRALIA:
WORLD CAPITAL OF DEADLIEST CREATURES?

The box jellyfish is just one of many unique and dangerous creatures that inhabit the land and waters of Australia.

Eastern Brown Snake

This foul-tempered reptile kills more people than any other snake in Australia. It's fast and aggressive, with powerful venom, and can kill within minutes. Its cousin, the western brown snake, isn't as mean or venomous, but one bite delivers three times more venom than the eastern brown, making it almost as dangerous.

Cassowary

These giant birds are shy,
but if they feel threatened,
they become extremely
dangerous. Cassowaries kill
by charging at their prey
at high speeds, leaping up,
and using the claws on
their feet to stab
and slice. Ouch!

NEXT
5km

Saltwater Crocodile

The world's largest
reptile grows to be as big
as 23 feet long and inhabits
brackish river waters. They lurk
beneath the water and launch
surprise attacks on
their prey.

POISONOUS VS.

A poisonous creature must be *eaten* or *touched* for its poison to affect its victim.

The SLOW LORIS is the only mammal on Earth that is both poisonous and venomous. It produces a toxin through a gland tucked on the inside of its elbows. It smears it on its babies to prevent them from being gobbled up by predators.

Poisonous and Venomous

Don't touch! This beautiful GOLDEN POISON ARROW FROG has enough poison to kill ten men. Its poison seeps into the skin and leads to a quick and painful death.

Poisonous

VENOMOUS

A venomous creature injects its toxin into its victim's bloodstream with fangs, stingers, or tentacles.

The sting of a DEATHSTALKER SCORPION is excruciating and deadly. Strangely, some people keep them as pets, which is not a good idea!

Venomous

Every year, snakebites kill as many as 90,000 people, with COBRAS and vipers causing the most deaths. India is the deadliest country for snakebites, with at least 11,000 deaths per year.

Venomous

WHAT IS THE DEADLIEST CREATURE ON EARTH? IS IT THE SHARK? THE LEOPARD? TURN THE PAGE TO FIND OUT.

AND THE WORLD'S DEADLIEST ANIMAL IS...

THE
MOSQUITO

THAT'S RIGHT. No creature on
Earth kills more people than
the tiny little mosquito. In
fact, mosquitoes cause more
deaths in the world than all
other animals combined. The
main reason is a disease called
malaria, which is spread by the
Anopheles mosquito. Malaria
kills approximately 725,000
people every year; the majority
are children living in Africa.

The Venomous Platypus?

The PLATYPUS isn't just fabulously strange looking, with its duck face and cuddly body. Male platypuses are venomous. On the inside of their hind feet, they have two sharp spurs that inject powerful venom. But don't worry. It's not *you* the platypus wants to hurt. Male platypuses use their venom on each other, when they are fighting over mates.

ACKNOWLEDGMENTS

I want to thank my friends at *Storyworks* for years of fun as we pursue our shared mission of creating amazing resources for kids and teachers.

I am deeply grateful for my talented colleague Allison Friedman, for the research assistance she provided on "The Volcano That Changed the World" and "The Bloodred Night."

Huge thanks to the many people I was lucky to work with on this book: Nancy Mercado, Elizabeth Krych, Joy Simpkins, Jessica Rozler, Yaffa Jaskoll, Jeffrey West, Cynthia Carris, and Cian O'Day.

Finally, huge love and thanks to Deb Dinger, who created the fact files and many ideas for the True Stories books. Over nearly twenty-five years of working together, Deb and I have forged a deep friendship and creative partnership. I couldn't have created these books without her.

MY SOURCES

Writing even a short nonfiction article requires countless hours of research. For each of the stories in this book, I relied on many sources, including books, newspaper and magazine articles, blogs, videos, maps, diaries, interviews, and face-to-face meetings.

Below are my main sources for each of the articles, including some books that you can explore.

SUMMER OF TERROR: THE SHARK ATTACKS OF 1916

Close to Shore: The Terrifying Shark Attacks of 1916, by Michael Capuzzo, New York: Crown Books, 2003

Twelve Days of Terror: A Definitive Investigation of the 1916 New Jersey Shark Attacks, by Richard G. Fernicola, M.D., Guilford, CT: The Lyons Press, 2001

Sharks and People: Exploring Our Relationship with the Most Feared Fish in the Sea, by Thomas Peschak, Chicago: The University of Chicago Press, 2013

Polio: An American Story, by David Oshinsky, Oxford, UK: Oxford University Press, 2005

"The Shark Attacks That Were the Inspiration for *Jaws*," by Megan Gambion, *Smithsonian*, 2012

"Cape Fear," by Alec Wilkinson, *The New Yorker*, September 9, 2013

Books you might like:

Close to Shore: The Terrifying Shark Attacks of 1916, by Michael Capuzzo, New York: Crown Books, 2003

I Survived the Shark Attacks of 1916, by Lauren Tarshis (that's me!), New York: Scholastic, 2010

THE BLOODRED NIGHT: THE GREAT PESHTIGO FIRE OF 1871

The Peshtigo Fire, an Eyewitness Account, by Reverend Peter Pernin, Madison, WI: Wisconsin Historical Society Press, 1999

Firestorm at Peshtigo: A Town, Its People, and the Deadliest Fire in American History, by Denise Gess and William Lutz, New York: Holt Paperbacks, 2003

Nature's Metropolis: Chicago and the Great West, by William Cronon, New York: W. W. Norton and Company, 1992

Under a Flaming Sky: The Great Hinckley Firestorm of 1894, by Daniel James Brown, New York: HarperCollins, 2007

Young Men and Fire, by Norman Maclean, Chicago: The University of Chicago Press, 1992

Fire on the Mountain: The True Story of the South Canyon Fire, by John M. McLean, New York: William Morrow, 1999

"Fire on the Mountain," by Brian Mockenhaupt, *The Atlantic,* June 2014

Books you might like:

The Great Peshtigo Fire: Stories and Science from America's Deadliest Firestorm, by Scott Knickelbine: Madison, WI: Wisconsin Historical Society Press, 2012

Little House on the Prairie, by Laura Ingalls Wilder, New York: Harper and Bros., 1941. Paperback reprint, New York: HarperCollins, 2008

THE VOLCANO THAT CHANGED THE WORLD: THE ERUPTION OF MOUNT TAMBORA, 1815

Tambora: The Eruption That Changed the World, by Gillen D'Arcy Wood, Princeton, NJ: The Princeton University Press, 2014

The Year Without Summer: 1816 and the Volcano That Darkened the World and Changed History, by William K. Klingaman and Nicholas P. Klingaman, New York: St. Martin's Press, 2013

The Little Ice Age: How Climate Made History 1300–1850, by Brian Fagan, New York: Basic Books, 2000

Eruptions That Shook the World, by Clive Oppenheimer, Cambridge, UK: Cambridge University Press, 2011

Krakatoa: The Day the World Exploded: August 27, 1883, by Simon Winchester, New York: Harper Perennial, 2003

Books you might like:

Eruption!: Volcanoes and the Science of Saving Lives, by Elizabeth Rusch, New York: HMH Books for Young Readers, 2013

Disaster Strikes #4: Volcano Blast, by Marlane Kennedy, New York: Scholastic, 2015

I Survived the Destruction of Pompeii, AD 79, by Lauren Tarshis, New York: Scholastic, 2014

THE INVISIBLE MONSTER: ONE GIRL'S ENCOUNTER WITH THE DEADLY BOX JELLYFISH

Stung!: On Jellyfish Blooms and the Future of the Ocean, by Lisa-ann Gershwin, Chicago: University of Chicago Press, 2013

"Jellyfish: The Next King of the Sea," by Abigail Tucker, *Smithsonian*, August 2010

"Australia's Box Jellyfish: A Killer Down Under," by William M. Hamner, *National Geographic*, Volume 186, Issue 1, February 1994

"Selected Jellyfish Hot Spots Around the World," The National Science Foundation, http://www.nsf.gov/news/special_reports/jellyfish/resources.jsp

"Should We Stop Using Vinegar to Treat Box Jelly Stings? Not Yet—Venom Experts Weigh in on Recent Study" by Christie Wilcox, *Science Sushi* (blog), *Discover*, April 9, 2014

PHOTO CREDITS

Scholastic Inc.; 104 top: The Granger Collection; 104 bottom: Bundy & Williams/Liljenquist Family Collection of Civil War Photographs/Library of Congress; 105 top: The Granger Collection; 105 bottom background: Edward S. Curtis Collection/Library of Congress; 105 bottom inset: Heyn/Corbis Images; 106 top: Everett Collection Historical/Alamy Images; 106 bottom: Songquan Deng/Shutterstock, Inc.; 107 top left: *New York Daily News* Archive/Getty Images; 107 top right: *New York Daily News* Archive/Getty Images; 107 bottom: Everett Collection Historical/Alamy Images; 108–109: Luka Lajst/iStockphoto; 110–111 background: Tarik Kizilkaya/iStockphoto; 110 top: All Canada Photos/Alamy Images; 110 bottom: Ric Francis/AP Images; 111 top: ZUMA Press, Inc/Alamy Images; 111 bottom: Christian Petersen/Getty Images; 112 top: Library of Congress; 112 bottom: parema/iStockphoto; 113: Justin Sullivan/Getty Images; 114 top: Time & Life Pictures/Getty Images; 114 bottom: Danita Delimont/Getty Images; 117: ANT Photo Library/Science Source; 120–121: ABC TV; 123 left: Robert Valentic/Nature Picture Library; 123 right: James van den Broek/Shutterstock, Inc.; 124: Kelvin Aitken/marinethemes.com; 126: Age fotostock/Superstock, Inc.; 128 left: Newspix/Getty Images; 128 right, 129 left: Courtesy Biopixel.tv; 129 right: Paul Sutherland/National Geographic Creative; 130: David Doubilet/National Geographic Creative; 133: Paul Sutherland/National Geographic Creative; 134: Rachael Shardlow/Newspix; 135: Paul Braven/APN/*Gladstone Observer*; 137 top left: Isselee/Dreamstime; 137 top right: Daniel Heuclin/Minden Pictures; 137 bottom: Joel Sartore/Getty Images; 138–139: Jeff Wildermuth/Getty Images; 140 top: ayzek/iStockphoto; 140 bottom: Kristian Bell/Dreamstime; 141 top left: Craig Dingle/iStockphoto; 141 top right: Kevin Schafer/Minden Pictures; 141 center: George Clerk/iStockphoto; 141 bottom: Andrew Burgess/Shutterstock, Inc.; 142–143 background: Visuals

ABOUT THE AUTHOR

Photo by David Dreyfuss

Lauren Tarshis's *New York Times*–bestselling I Survived series tells stories of young people and their resilience and strength in the midst of unimaginable disasters. Lauren has brought her signature warmth and exhaustive research to topics such as the September 11 attacks, the destruction of Pompeii, Hurricane Katrina, and the bombing of Pearl Harbor, among others. In addition to being the editor of Scholastic's *Storyworks* magazine and group editorial director for language arts for Scholastic classroom magazines, Lauren is also the author of the critically acclaimed novels *Emma-Jean Lazarus Fell Out of a Tree* and *Emma-Jean Lazarus Fell in Love*. She lives in Westport, Connecticut, and can be found online at www.laurentarshis.com.

ABOUT STORYWORKS

Storyworks is an award-winning classroom magazine read by more than 700,000 kids in grades three to six. Combining thrilling stories and articles across the genres plus amazing teacher support and online resources, *Storyworks* is a beloved and powerful language arts resource.

For more information go to:
www.scholastic.com/storyworks

I SURVIVED

TRUE STORIES: FIVE EPIC DISASTERS

REAL KIDS. REAL DISASTERS.

From the author of the *New York Times*–bestselling I Survived series come five harrowing true stories of survival, featuring real kids in the midst of epic disasters.

From a group of students surviving the 9.0 earthquake that set off a historic tsunami in Japan, to a boy nearly frozen on the prairie in 1888, these unforgettable kids lived to tell tales of unimaginable destruction—and, against all odds, survival.

THE JOPLIN TORNADO, 2011

A DESTRUCTIVE FORCE IS ABOUT TO HIT THE CITY OF JOPLIN . . .

Eleven-year-old Dexter has always wanted to see a tornado. So when he gets the incredible opportunity to go storm chasing with the famous Dr. Norman Gage, he has to say yes! Dr. Gage is the host of *Tornado Mysteries*, the show that Dex and his older brother, Jeremy, watched every night until Jeremy joined the US Navy SEALs and left Joplin.

Dex certainly knows how deadly tornadoes can be, but this one isn't heading toward Joplin, and wouldn't it be great to have a brave and exciting story of his own to tell Jeremy when he comes home? But when the tornado shifts direction, Dexter's bravery is about to get seriously tested . . .

THE GREAT CHICAGO FIRE, 1871

COULD AN ENTIRE CITY REALLY BURN TO THE GROUND?

Oscar Starling never wanted to come to Chicago. But then Oscar finds himself not just in the heart of the big city, but in the middle of a terrible fire! No one knows exactly how it began, but one thing is clear: Chicago is like a giant powder keg about to explode.

An army of firemen is trying to help, but this fire is a ferocious beast that wants to devour everything in its path, including Oscar! Will Oscar survive one of the most famous and devastating fires in history?

THE DESTRUCTION OF POMPEII, AD 79

THE BEAST BENEATH THE MOUNTAIN IS RESTLESS...

No one in the bustling city of Pompeii worries when the ground trembles beneath their feet. Everyone knows that the beast under the mountain Vesuvius, high above the city, wakes up angry sometimes — and always goes back to sleep.

But Marcus is afraid. He knows something is terribly wrong — and his father, who trusts science more than mythical beasts, agrees. When Vesuvius explodes into a cloud of fiery ash and rocks fall from the sky like rain, will they have time to escape — and survive the complete destruction of Pompeii?

THE NAZI INVASION, 1944

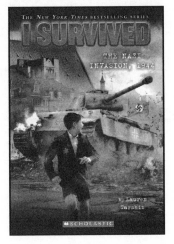

ONE OF THE DARKEST PERIODS IN HISTORY...

In a Jewish ghetto, Max Rosen and his sister Zena struggle to live after their father is taken away by the Nazis. With barely enough food to survive, the siblings make a daring escape from Nazi soldiers into the nearby forest.

Max and Zena are brought to a safe camp by Jewish resistance fighters. But soon, bombs are falling all around them. Can Max and Zena survive the fallout of the Nazi invasion?

THE
JAPANESE
TSUNAMI, 2011

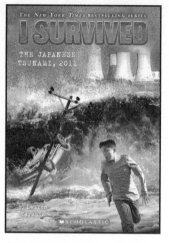

THE DISASTER FELT
AROUND THE WORLD

Visiting his dad's hometown in Japan four months after his father's death would be hard enough for Ben. But one morning the pain turns to fear: First, a massive earthquake rocks the quiet coastal village, nearly toppling his uncle's house. Then the ocean waters rise and Ben and his family are swept away—and pulled apart—by a terrible tsunami.

Now Ben is alone, stranded in a strange country a million miles from home. Can he fight hard enough to survive one of the most epic disasters of all time?

I SURVIVED

THE BATTLE OF GETTYSBURG, 1863

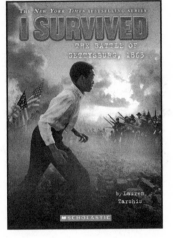

THE BLOODIEST BATTLE IN AMERICAN HISTORY IS UNDER WAY...

It's 1863, and Thomas and his little sister, Birdie, have fled the farm where they were born and raised as slaves. Following the North Star, looking for freedom, they soon cross paths with a Union soldier. Everything changes: Corporal Henry Green brings Thomas and Birdie back to his regiment, and suddenly it feels like they've found a new home. Best of all, they don't have to find their way north alone — they're marching with the army.

But then orders come through: The men are called to battle in Pennsylvania. Thomas has made it so far . . . but does he have what it takes to survive Gettysburg?

THE ATTACKS OF SEPTEMBER 11, 2001

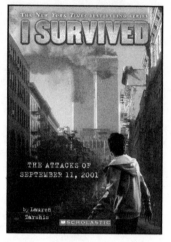

A DAY THAT WILL CHANGE THE NATION...

The only thing Lucas loves more than football is his dad's friend Benny, a firefighter and former football star. He taught Lucas the game and helps him practice. So when Lucas's parents decide football is too dangerous and he needs to quit, Lucas *has* to talk to his biggest fan.

On a whim, Lucas takes the train to the city instead of the bus to school. It's a bright, beautiful day in New York. But just as Lucas arrives at the firehouse, everything changes ... and nothing will ever be the same again.